PUBLISHING COMPANY

REACH THE PRESS

PRESENT

GOD HAS A PURPOSE
AND A PLAN FOR ME

AND
THE STORM IS OVER NOW

By: *Michelle T. Duplessis*

1

Reach The Press Publishing
14051Belle Chasse Blvd Unit 213
Laurel, Maryland 20707

Printed in the United States of America

Introduction

To Michelle memoir a collection of memories as she writes about her own life. Michelle was putting one foot in front of the other, making one mistake after another. Not having parental spiritual guidance during childhood. After reaching adulthood realizing that she did not know God and was not walking in Gods will; was a turning point in Michelle life and she made an effort to learn about Jesus Christ and live her life according to the Word of God.

GOD HAS A PURPOSE
AND A PLAN FOR ME

This book is devoted to all the women and men who step out on their own and made mistakes because they did not wait on God for direction. I made a whole lot of mistakes, I hurt and was hurt by a lot of people along the way, and however, I didn't know how to love or be love. The decisions I made, of course, affected my life significantly and if this book can help one person I will be so grateful, what we have to learn is that we all have a purpose, and I didn't feel I had one I felt like a complete failure, but that's just how the enemy wants us to feel.

Surprise! we all have someone in our home who are going through something. From sexual abuse, drugs, being abused as a child or seeing our mom being abused. Someone suffering from depression, which all of these are a form of spirit that we are dealing with, because we don't wrestle with flesh, Ephesians 6:12 tells us that, For we wrestle not against flesh and blood, but against principalities, against powers, against the rulers of the darkness of this world, against spiritual wickedness in high places. I felt lost a lot but I was because I was around all the wrong people, we need to go where there is positive energy where you can *be and feel reciprocated, celebrated and appreciated, not tolerated, not made to feel unwelcome and unloved or an outcast. We have to realize that everybody is not going to celebrate your success with you, some are trying to figure out… how did she/he make it through that? It's because God has a purpose and a plan for your life and no matter how many times you fail GET BACK UP!!!!! As you give your life to Him, you can find your Divine purpose.*

PSALM 20:4

*Grant thee according to
thine own heart, and fulfill
all thy counsel.*

In Loving Memories

Memories are the treasures
that I lock deep within my
heart for my Mother. She is no
longer with me but the time
she told me that she love me is
forever a part of my thoughts.
We had some unpleastant
times but most important is her
wanting me to know that she
loved me. That moment in time
was a gift from my Mother that
I will always cherish. Gone from
my presents but always in my
memories.......

My Mother

Glenda Leblanc Smith

Table of Contents

Table of Contents

Dedication

This book is dedicated to everyone who inspired me to write it, especially my kids and grandkids who has had such an impact on my life. Through all my bad and good decisions, and all the mistakes I have made along the way. You all have embraced me in your own way, and I appreciate that so much. But one person that was my rock, she treated me like her own daughter she was indeed my mom, my friend, who loved me like no other. A love so genuine and sweet and unconditional, with all my flaws no matter what we went through she, never turned her back on me.

Dedication

When a lot of people did she stood by me, she loved me like no one ever has, I have never experienced this kind of love before, my Mama Nell, Mrs. Ora Nell Tanks my angel now resting with my heavenly father.

Thank You

I would also like to say a special thanks to my sisters Sandra Charles and Johnnie Williams, you have inspired me so much, I got what I always wanted... sisters sent by God who always been there for my kids and me every step of the way. Words cannot express what you mean to me and the impact you have had on my life, thank you from the bottom of my heart. Sabrina Blanchard, my lifesaver, my inspiration, my adopted mom, you are amazing I do not know how I would have made it through high school or where I would be without you, you gave me what I needed some tough love, and still nurtured me with unconditional love as if I was your own, thank you.

Thank You

My beautiful Brittney my friend they say you're not supposed to be your kid's friend, but you are just that my best friend and my rock the older we get, the sweeter the love I have for you gets, you are a beautiful person inside and out.

Thank You

You are a wonderful mom and wife and let's not forget Chad I could not ask for a better son in law, and I just love you guys so much, Brits you make life worth living every time I thought about giving up I see your face, I love you. My kids all have something unique about them. That I just love so much, Brits, of course, does not give up until she has achieved her goals. That's how she was able to finish nursing school with kids while baking her cakes. Carey Jr, has always been an achiever playing the tough guy while being a great provider and husband and father but he really has a heart of gold. While I was going through my storm it was him and his wife that open up their home to me, he didn't ask me for anything he says mama I just want you to get on your feet. I was having a tough time when I first got there I thought God was punishing me for the things that I had done in my past, and it was Lil Carey that shared the word with me and encouraged and let me know that's not how God did things, so for that I'm so grateful. Christopher, aka Mr. Chris, was my affectionate one always laying on my back always just loving as a kid so sweet and now a great dad to his girls so proud of you Mr. Chris. Brandon, anybody who knows snuffy knows he gives the best hugs ever and that's what I miss most about him being far away from me those sweet hugs, and he's still my baby.   To my sisters and brothers, I have

Thank You

learned so much from you guys thanks.
My friend my kid's father Carey L Tanks
Sr… since high school I love you.
Although things didn't work out I still
appreciate you, you were my best friend,
my husband. Things were not always
perfect between us but that's not what I
will remember the most, in the beginning,
I was trying to figure out what I did to
deserve such a sweet, gentle, loving man,
I love you always.

Thank You

Prophet Michael Ayers Sr., I don't know where to begin... you have always been there for my kids and me. You're a real man of GOD who has always loved GODs people and wanted to help in any way you can, and I'm forever grateful. You taught me how to believe in myself again, how to love myself and most of all how to love and trust GOD and seek him for everything, you have helped me to develop a beautiful relationship with GOD. Thank you for never sugar coating anything, it was much needed, thanks for being stern with me, some of the things you said to me were hard hurtful and tough but much needed, it only made me stronger. Thanks, I love you.

Thank You

My leader and pastor Dr. Herbert Rowe, I was wounded when I came to you, and you and your wife loved on me, and for that I'm grateful, I learned so much from you, your love for GODs people is genuinely unconditional, I miss you and love you.

Waiting on my Soulmate

Waiting on my mate Tall dark and handsome, that is what we say we like, but a man after Gods own heart now that is mister right, I will know him when he comes, he is so smooth and polite and walks with such authority. The fear of God he has, yes, he will treat me like royalty. He knows what it means to open doors, help you in and out of cars, and up and down stairs, and yes, he

will even brush my hair, So, you go
on settling for a little of nothing,
thinking you got you some kind of
treat, but the word says a man that
does not work does not eat.
You see lights, water, rent, bills
won't be our worry, my mate and I
will work together and take full
authority. I will walk with him and
support him and be his backbone,
I will not belittle him, and you see a
man needs to know he is King of his
throne. We will be able to sit and
talk and work out our problems as
they come, we will pray for each

other, I will be his, and he will be my covering. We will pray and worship God together, it will be no such thing as let's stay home from church because of bad weather. He will push and motivate me and make me feel so safe and secure, I will have to go to God and ask, is this man real? So, guys sorry no you can not take me out, call me up, or even hold my hand, this means no dinner, movie, nothing! Sorry, I must take a stand.

You see this my season, and the devil
…he is looking for any reason, he
wants me to miss out on what God
has for me, but I won't be moved, I
am standing like that old palm tree.
So yes, I am waiting on my mate, and
until then there is no such thing as
it's just a friendly date and my God
will let me know when he comes and
what he will say, yep that will be the
perfect date.

I am saving myself waiting on my mate just as I stated because without my God I never would have made it.
Dated January 5, 2009

Because I believed in second chances.

By: Michelle T. Duplessis

A Little Girl

I wrote a poem to express how I was feeling when I started realizing that this was a spiritual thing and not a physical thing. Helpless, a little girl born into this world of trials and tribulations. Not knowing what her future holds, a lot of big girls' situations. Her early years she should be in her mothers' arms being loved nurtured, adored, cherished and protected. Instead, she finds herself all alone in big girl's situations and very much rejected.

All she wanted is for her mother to hold her and tell her she loves her, that she will keep her safe and out of harm's way. Instead, she allows the enemy to abuse, use, strip, defile, and violate, shame and take away her innocence and still, she let him stay. Stay to destroy, takeover, ruin, sweet little innocent lives, too little to fight back, too young to know how don't have a clue any direction. One thing for sure she was not our hedge of protection. Now sweet sixteen hating men and how she's been violated never wanting ever to give them another chance.

Never did anything like a normal kid,
never even had her first dance. The
older she gets, the more bitter she never
becomes really learning how to love,
forgive or let go of her past, feeling that
one day she is going to miss out on her
one chance to really dance. Too
stubborn to let go enough to love and be
loved, trying to make all her pain go
away in alcohol and smoking weed.
Not realizing that the devil is planting
a terrible seed. Now her faith lies only
in God, he has delivered and set her free
from much of her hurt and pain,

He said I have carried you all your life
I have never left you my child and
when you called on me, I came, where
this girl is now and how is her life?
Can she love or do she even think
twice? Yes, God told her I have a little
something for you it's just a small
token, I just want you to know my
child you were bruised but not broken
where this sweet little girl is, how is
she now? She is stronger, learning to
love, forgive, and trust entirely on God,
you see, well, you just take a good look
because that little girl was me.

By: Michelle T. Duplessis

Chapter I

HOW DID WE ALL GET HERE!!!!!

1 Corinthians 2:9 says, but it is written, Eyes hath not seen nor ears heard neither has entered into the heart of man the things which God had prepared for them that love him. Let me make something obvious, and that is, this is my opinion my story my testimony, and we all have one, and we don't have to agree on everything, and I'm sure some will and some won't but however it's not meant to offend anyone. Sometimes we need a song in our heart or scripture in our heart to keep our

mind stayed on Jesus. Sometimes that's the only way we can make it. I knew from a little Girl that God was very real, our neighbors were Jehovah witness and I remember going with my parents to the Kingdom Hall and being taught about Jehovah with them, and sing this song I loved, from house to house from door to door… I loved that song. I lived with my mom and stepdad and my sister and five brothers, now what I didn't know then that I know now was that we all had a great calling on our lives and because of it the enemy would attack us at a very young age. Growing up was very difficult for us, we grew up in a house full of chaos and confusion, dysfunctional and very abusive, why? Because my parents didn't really know God themselves, and how to pray or operate in the spirit, and because of that we all suffered even them because they were not raised in the word how could they act in the spirit and recognized Satan when he showed up. You cannot pass something on to your children that you were not taught unless someone presented it to you. So, I hold nothing in my heart for my parents because they didn't know how to fight for us, now I'm sure some reading my story may feel that some of the things they did they knew were wrong and I am sure that's true. In their defense without the spirit of God living on the inside of you, how can you fight the enemy with no power? My family has always been full of division from as far as I can remember, with my siblings, I can remember it was always a division with some of us, some of us were never close.

 I guess we have done the best we could considering our childhood. II Corinthians 3:17 says, now, the Lord is that Spirit: and where the Lord is, there is Liberty. I truly believe because the spirit of God was not in our home we didn't know to love each other and express ourselves to one another without it being some kind of chaos. I love my family very much, but there was a time that I did not want to be around some of them. I did not know why at the time, but it was because I didn't know how to love or war in the spirit. I was battling against spirits, not flesh. I can remember when somethings were happening to me, and I didn't understand why or what they were doing to me, I didn't think I was a naughty child, I just could not figure out why was this happening, was it because I was bad or good? I just could not make sense of it I just knew it was not right. However, I do have good memories when I was young everything was not all bad. It just seems like some of my brothers were treated worse than anybody in our home. I know a lot of people may ask why I'm writing about this now. It's not to offend anyone it's to help me heal it's a part of my testimony it's helping me with my deliverance. We needed Christ in the home, and our house is not the only home went through this. People are just afraid to talk about it worrying about what others are going to say. Not realizing that people need to hear your story and know that they were not alone. They can make it out of the situation also, and most of all stop covering up stuff and expose the enemy for who he really is and walk in your victory because you are not alone.

Chapter 2

THE SEED WAS PLANTED

I remember knowing that there was
a God Just by the feeling I got going
to the Kingdom Hall with my mom
neighbor. I really liked it there, you
see God always has a ram in the
bush. I don't care what religion she
was I still got something from her,
and I remembered some of the
things she taught me. I would
sometimes pray mostly when I knew
I was in trouble of course, and I did
not want a whipping, or even while I
was getting one I would call on
Jehovah God, and that would really
make my mom mad. I understand
now that my mom was not saved she

did not know Christ at the time. She was raising us, I can't stress this enough because I want to make clear to everybody that my mom could not help us if she could not help herself, so I cannot hold anything against her, and I want to make that very clear. I love my mom and regret the way I treated her when I became older I am so sorry about that, I would go months without talking to her just holding onto anger. Let me just say I was looking at some photos of her old and young and my mom was beautiful… Before she married my stepdad she was married to my dad, they married very young, and I think my dad just had a lot of growing up to do. I never really got a chance to know him I met him and been around him a few times, but he always managed to drift in and out of my life. When possible, I do call him and check on him when he is reachable. I do not know what really happened between him and my mother. I do know that when we choose our mates instead of waiting on God to send them to us, we pay dearly for disobedience. Being impatient I had several fail marriages. I believe because my mom chose her mates we suffered and she did as well. Now reaching adulthood myself, I understand her also hurt because we were not the only victims she was as well. Now a seed was planted, and the whole house suffered. I do remember my stepdad being nice sometimes, but most of the time to me it was a living hell especially for my older brothers who were not his, he always seemed to find fault in everything they did he look for a reason not to provide anything for them or to beat them or put them out. I know we couldn't have always been punished, but it really seemed like they were always punished. My brothers could not eat, go outside, locked in a room for hours, it was just crazy. What you must remember is that nobody was saved in that house. Being so afraid, I hid a cup in my closet in case I had to use the bathroom. Its funny I was never able to talk about this before I just held a lot of bitterness in my heart for my entire family until I realized that it was not our fault, that it was the work of the enemy. This is my deliverance this is my testimony, and I feel my healing and deliverance even as I write this. I often wondered why my dad never came to get us or checked on us, did he even know what we were going through and just did not care!

I was in elementary school sleeping outside as a punishment with my other siblings, I was so scared I do not know how long we were out there, but it seemed like forever, and it was dark. I remember my neighbor would sometimes give me a peanut butter and jelly sandwich. When we were out there, and it was good too, and she would always talk about this place called paradise on earth for good people, and I knew I wanted to live there when she would have bible study at our house, and it was nice, but soon things were back to normal. It actually seemed worst to me, we were beaten with anything my mom could get her hands on, cords, brooms, spoons, and knives anything she picked up. I did not want to bathe because my skin would sting so bad because I sometimes had cuts, sometimes I did not want to go to school because I was so marked up, we all were.

As a kid, I was greedy even though I was small and to me, the worst punishment of all was not, being able to eat, oh my goodness. I would be so happy to eat or go to school to eat oh yeah. Honestly how many people do you know that are going through this that you can help with your testimony, I hear about it all the time, look at all the kids that are being killed today, being starved, beating, stop covering things up and tell your story saints we all have one. Now with all the turmoil that we were going through we witness each other go through this and for me, it brought about shame and distance. All the chaos and uproar we had been going through the enemy used it to destroy and tear down our family. We watched and witnessed each other go through so much we became angry bitter and hateful, or should I speak for myself. My mom had failed as a mother to protect us, and we all suffered even her. No one was happy, the enemy had accomplished his mission, and we all were victims of abuse, physical, mental and even sexual for some of us. Yes, I remember going by my stepdad family house. Where

one of his nephews would constantly
put his hands in my underwear. He
would rub me so hard till it would
hurt and I would be so sore. Then he
would tell me if I said anything he
would let his big dogs bite me. He
had two of them I will never forget
them I was terrified of them as a
child. I did, however, tell my sister
who told my mom who beat the crap
out of us both, we never told my
mom anything after that well I know
I did not. The beatings were much
worse than the molestation or sexual
abuse. My mom had two sons for
my stepdad who was apparently
treated much better than we were.

As a child, I did not like them very much because of it because I did not understand it all at that time being a child. Becoming an adult, I grew to love them the older I got, and they are so special to me because they were not responsible for anything that happened to us they were kids. That is why it is so important not to be unequally yoked and to know and trust God and wait on your mate. Which I fail to do, God will not send you someone who will treat your kids different from theirs, and I'm not saying you will not go through some things as a Christian, but it will be a lot easier if we wait on the

Lord. I had two failed marriages because I did what I wanted to do when each time God said to wait and my second marriage God said flat out NO. I listened to my friends and some family, and my kids and I suffered because of it. Going back to my childhood so now the enemy planted a seed of division in our house but we did not know that then, well I didn't. My sister wanted to protect my little brothers from everything, she was crazy about them from the time they were born, and she did not like nobody fussing or spanking them she was their protector. Although we were never close, she was always there if you needed a way out a place to stay she was there, she hated the abuse we all endured. I don't remember a real closeness with any of my siblings. Really, I learned what family was like when I married Carey and met his family. His sisters became my sisters, and his mom became my mom. What I discovered was what a real family looked like, and I had never seen that you see Satan had planted a seed in our lives at a young age with parents who were not saved or didn't really know God. They didn't know how to pray and destroy some yolks, and we were exposed to so much negativity that we did not know how to show or express love to one another. We lied on each other, and fought against each other, we did not see genuine love so we could not display it to one another. I really feel my oldest brothers suffered the most, and because of it, my brothers began to really act out and get in trouble. My stepdad even had my brother put in a boy's home, and that was to me a significant turning point in his life because my mom allowed it she did not protect him. We needed her to defend us to love us something she did not know how to do. I loved going to school (when there weren't any whelps on me), some of my friends were really nice to me although I did not know how to be a friend to them.

They had no idea what was going on in my house, but anyway at school, I had lunch, and I could play outside and be a kid, but I hated going home. So now there was hatred, bitterness, envy, hurt and jealousy and a feeling of betrayal in my heart to name a few. I would say the devil planted his seed in our house to destroy our family, and mission accomplished at that time.

The seed was planted
Continues

I remember moving into another house, but things only got worse because my brothers were older. My stepdad knew he could not continue pushing them around so like I said earlier he sends them to a boy's home he put my oldest in Milne boys home and my other brother was in a place called Scotlandville. My brothers started getting into trouble by stealing food and clothes, and it just continued, they had no one to help them they were teenagers no

clothes to go to school no one to
feed them and no place to stay my
parents put them out very young.
They never had a chance at life and
began to make bad decisions. My
sister help all of us when she could,
but she was young, but she opened
her doors to all of us, but who was
really going to motivate us?
And encourage us to do better. My
mom's first child to graduate, he
could not walk across the stage with
his classmates, his big day and he
missed it, why I am not really sure.
I will not go into every detail, but I
will say these two things that
bothered me the most that I never

forgot was watching my brother head being stumped on the floor by my stepdad, and mom checking his ears for blood after it. My other brother head being knocked through a window and a spoon being thrown at him that struck his head. I will never forget those events and the hurts they faced being abused by two people who were supposed to protect them it was heartbreaking. I didn't feel no love there so how you can display it. So, I'm sure the boys were a lot safer in a boy's home or jail than living at home, and they could eat, or that's what I thought.

You see the lord is our protection
and we as parents with the help of
the Lord is our kid's protection.

Genesis 15:1
Says …The Lord is my protective
shield and my abundant
compensation!

He rewards faith! … I didn't know
these scriptures back then, but if I
did, I would have used them against
the enemy. One of my favorites is,
Job 1:10, I pray a hedge of
protection around me and my house!
Thank you for blessing the work of
my hands and increasing my
substance!

This is my prayer for my house,
Psalm 18:29 says, God, with you, I
can run through a troop and leap
over a wall! Nothing can stop me!
Prayer and protection are what we
needed at that time. I really do not
know how I made it through high
school, I was mean to people who
were nice to me. I lied all the time
just to fit in, I became someone else
who really did not care much about
life, what had happened to me made
me feel so empty inside I just could
care less about anything. The devil
was having a ball with my family. I
remember my mom had surgery. I
helped her, and she told me things

were going to get better. She always said it, but she looked really sad this time like she was hurting herself and not just from her surgery. I thought maybe this woman that I called mom might just like me a little, but that didn't last long. I graduated with the help of my Godmother Sabrina Blanchard she took me in and put me through my senior year, and I made it, my mom never came to see me walk across the stage, but I had my sister and Sabrina, and all Tanks were there my mama Nell. Again, what is this book about? My healing, my deliverance, my testimony, not to offend no one. If you find it hurtful or hard to read, try living it. I think people need to know the importance of going ahead of God, it means everyone suffers, hurt people hurt people. I'm sure if my parents had known Christ our life would have been very different. Middle school I loved it, but high school was more trying for me, but I made it. I met some really lovely people I made some new friends that I soon lost, they didn't want to be my friend anymore, why? Because I didn't know how to be a real friend to them, I was not taught that there was no loyalty or real friendship in my house. Therefore, I kept to myself a lot in middle school, I couldn't explain to everyone what was really going on in my house I was too embarrassed, so yes, I acted out and was rebellious. Psalms 18:2 says, the Lord is my rock. He is solid and does not change. He is my fortress, surrounding me with protection. He is my deliverer, always making way for me. My God, My Refuge! As kids, we did not know how to war in the spirit, or use scriptures in prayer, or even how to pray, but God is so good, yes, we all made some bad choices, but God still saw us through and again healing some of us.

I lost one of my brothers, and one is incarcerated, but I'm always grateful that God kept us. I remember I would start trouble at school with the other kids, I would take money from my parents, and the whole time the devil was planting a seed in my life. I do not know how I even made it through middle or high school because I really did not focus on my work I was wondering what was going to happen when we got home. I would be wondering if my brothers where ok or even my sister, you just didn't know. I did not know how to love. I remember reading John 3:16, For God so loved the world.

That he gave his only begotten son, that whosoever believeth in him should not perish, but have everlasting life. I have eternal life! You did not send Jesus to condemn me, but to save me, and I thank you for that Jesus!!! That is some kind of love, he gave his only son for you and me. Now we had become young adults my sister married, and she has met this man called Jesus, and my sister always said if she ever got her own house none of us would be sleeping in cars or homeless again. I never slept in a car, but my brothers did. My sister kept her word she helps all of us out at some point in our life. My sister also, led me to Christ, and that was the best thing that could have ever happened to me, I still did not know how to love or be loved, but things look a little better. When I got saved I started reading scriptures like Matthews 5:44 But I say unto you, love your enemies, bless them that curse you, do good to them that hate you, and pray for them which despitefully use you and persecute you. Now I'm trying to figure out how will I do that because I had no love in my heart for my parents and a few other people that had hurt me. Now God is telling me to love them!! This did not seem fair to me, so I began to pray for Guidance, and I came across Psalms25:4-5, Show me thy ways, O LORD; teach me thy paths, lead me in thy truth, and guide me: for thou art the God of my salvation; on thee do I wait all day. I was determined that one day I was going to be free from this hurt and pain because I found out I was hindering my own blessings. *Then I read Psalms 37:24, the steps of a good man are ordered by the LORD: and he delights in his ways.* Order my steps oh Lord I need direction and correction.

I realized I had to forgive, so I started praying for forgiveness, and I began to read, Romans 12:21, be not overcome of evil, but overcome evil with good. I needed to meditate on that scripture because bitterness and revenge were in my heart. I want to be set free from that, so I prayed and read my word and believed God for change. I was not totally serious or ready to give God my all because now I'm grown and now I think I knew it all and determined not to let anyone hurt me again. Married with my own kids and family not really having a relationship with mom or my siblings because my heart was still hardening about a lot of things, and I had an unforgiving heart, and I still did not know how to love or be a real friend to anyone every time I think I got a friend, the enemy would remind me of my past and what people had done to me not what I had done to them? But God spoke to my heart even then, and I knew it was God, and I also knew I did not want to go to hell. So, I begin to fast and pray, I found myself praying a lot, but no matter how much I prayed the bitterness and anger and vengeance was still in my heart. I married my high school sweetheart the love of my life, and I could not love him or let him love me because I was waiting for him to hurt our kids or me. I did not trust him. I trusted no one, and I remember changing my daughter's diaper. My husband walked in, and I flipped out on him, and he just looked at me, he said that he was her father and that I was crazy, and he said what kind of childhood did you have because we don't have this kind of crazy stuff going on at my house. I did not know what to say to him I was too ashamed to tell him my story. I'm all over the place with this, and I know it, but I'm writing it as it comes to my remembrance. Must I say Carey Tanks Sr was the most loving affectionate man I've ever met till this day, he was a fantastic dad and a great father until he became sick I will say?

Chapter 3

GIVING THE ENEMY ACCESS TO YOU!!!

Be careful what you speak out of your mouth. I remember saying how much I hated men. I would never date one because they were so evil. They are all the same, and Satan knew and listened to everything I said. So what did he do...send nothing but homosexuals my way. Before I married my first husband I dated women, they were so much nicer to me. How many of you know that is how the enemy comes. Then I was trying to figure out how did I get here? I went to church one night with my sister and the man of God called me up and said God said to choose this day who I would serve. That God was not pleased with my lifestyle, so I pretended not to know what he was talking about and he whispered it in my ear that homosexual spirit, and I just cried I knew it was God because I told no one what I was doing. That day I made a change for the better but it was hard for me because I just wanted someone to love me and I had not experienced that but except with this girl. I had started dating my husband and still battling with this. But everything changed when I got baptized I felt clean and free I went home in the bathroom and cried and cried because I was free and I felt different I knew God had done something with me at this point, I was happy, but that was short lived because soon after I married everything was going wrong again, my wonderful husband was on drugs... I was heartbroken, but I did stay long enough to have our four amazing kids, but I started partying drinking smoking and going back to clubs to try not to think about what was happening at home being alone a failed marriage. I was very protective of my kids I didn't want anybody to put them through what I had endured as a child, but spiritually and emotionally I was doing the same things my mom did us, not protecting them or their anointing. I could not pray for them or cover them because I was out of the will of God myself, now my marriage is in serious trouble I cannot pray for my husband or me and he using drugs and now were in divorce court, I feel like I failed.

Now my brother is staying with me, and his friend is there all the time, and I'm not partying anymore. I'm home and back in church, and his friend is spending time with us cooking and cleaning, so yes, we get married. I never really loved him, and he knew it he said it first. I was so unhappy, and God gave me a warning before I married him. He showed me in a dream that we were at the altar and right after we said I do. His face disfigured and turned into a demon and he said b----h, I got you now. I knew he was not for me, and he was good to me, and my kids in the beginning and the enemy job is to destroy right, and blind you from the truth, and when you out of the will of God he reigns, so once again I'm miserable. I made some very poor choices in my life that would affect my kids as well, but I did not know what to do. I was so confused. Well, that ended in a divorce, and unlike my first husband whom I loved and missed so much. I felt a weight being lifted off me this time. I remember being sad about my divorce from my first husband and crying all the time. This was different, and I promised myself that I would wait on God if ever again.

During that time, I was going through a divorce from my second husband my stepdad passes. The next year we divorced, and the next month my mom passed. Let me say, that my ex-husband help take care of my mom, He cooked cleaned took her to her appointments for everything he was there he was a big help with her. I'm grateful for the good things he did. I wanted people to think I was so happy, we traveled I got whatever I wanted, but I was hurting the whole time. I said no more doing it my way nope.

To many time we as women stay in marriages for security, let God be our everything. I began to read and fast and pray a lot, I had become hungry for the word, and one day I was in church, and my Pastor told me she saw me getting married, I found that strange because I was not dating and didn't have any desire to do so. A few months passed, and I started dating a minister who said God told him I was his wife! His wife had died of cancer, not so, God said in his word that he will give wisdom to anyone who asks for it!

When I met this man, I began to pray for wisdom, and the Lord began to show me quickly that he was playing with God, his heart was not right, and he told so many different lies it was clear he was not serious, Proverbs 3:5 Trust in the LORD with all thine heart: and lean not unto thine own understanding. I was learning to trust God for everything, not a man and I did not want another failed relationship, and the lies he told even on his own parents I knew he could do the same to me. He just wanted someone to have sex with. I just wanted out, and God made an easy way for me.

Ecclesiastes 7:12, for wisdom is a defense, and money is a defense: but Excellency of knowledge is, that wisdom giveth life to them that have it. Jesus wants us to live a victorious life that's what I intended to do if I had to do alone. I'm special to God, and all that I went through was so he could get the glory, my suffering was not in vain, my mistakes were not in vain. I grew from it, and I learned from it, and I thank God for it the good the bad and the ugly. Matthew 5:13, says ye are the salt of the earth: but if the salt has lost his savor, wherewith shall it be salted?

It is thenceforth good for nothing,
but to be cast out, and to be trodden
under foot of men. That scripture
helped me with my confidence. I
began to walk by faith (for we walk
by faith, not by sight:) 2 Corinthians
5:7 I was developing a relationship
with God for myself and soon I did
not have to call people for prayer I
was able to pray for myself and
believe by faith I had what I asked
for. God was also increasing my
faith. I'm still young and have my
life to live, and things are looking
better. I and the kids moved to
Slidell, Louisiana and I started over,
but you know the devil will come

again, that is what happens. Satan showed up at my door saying he made a mistake and God showed him and confirmed to him that I was his wife... I was like devil get behind me, I was not falling for that again you lust demon. God has made me wiser, you see every relationship I was In I learned from them and Satan cannot trick me again. I have learned from my mistakes which have made me stronger. I also, learned from that relationship with the preacher that Satan knows that bible very well, he can quote scriptures and preach a sermon, and manipulate very well, therefore, none of that impresses me when I meet someone like that, I had to learn to pray for myself for wisdom and understanding which God began to give me very clear. That relationship was a setup by the enemy to destroy me, but God set me free from another disaster. I remember I had just had major surgery and was in the hospital and this preacher… got in my hospital bed and began to have intercourse with me while I was lying on my side, I was in so much pain I could not move I was shocked, I just laid there I was cut across my stomach and also inside my stomach, but he did not care. When I got home, and he brought me back, I felt dirty and violated I never told anyone. I just started pulling away from him and my pastor she kept telling me he was a great man, so I started pulling away from her and her church. I had no room for error or to be in a ministry that could not help me. If you love me respect me and that was not love, so he asked me one day to give him time to get it together that he did not want to hurt me or disappoint me, and six months later he was married.

And he was still emailing me that he thinks he made a big mistake, I never answered not once.

God is so good he kept me and set me free from that relationship which was sent to destroy me. Life is about choices, we live, and we learn, and we as Christians must share our testimonies to help others, it's not to hurt people or make them uncomfortable but to help them. It's about letting someone else know that they are not alone, that you have been there too and God can bring you out of any situation. How can you help others if you haven't been there?

One thing I tried to do was let my kids know everything that was going on in my life, I did not want anyone else to tell them about my past I felt that was my job. I have great kids I am so proud of them, and as parents we want our kids to do better than we did, and my kids have done just that, they are amazing parents. I made a lot of mistakes raising them, and I hope they can one day forgive me. I was young and headstrong and foolish and like my parents not operating in the spirit not really knowing God or how to pray. At that time in my life playing with God thinking I was going to get away with it. God is so merciful and forgiving, his mercy and grace are unbelievable, but his love is something I cannot explain. When I realized just how much God loves me that he died for me, his love is unconditional, a love I never felt before from anybody, and that is when I learned how to love my friends, family, kids, and myself, that is when I wanted to make a real change.

Chapter 4

I THOUGHT I HAD IT TOGETHER

Now I have peace I can hear God a lot better and focus on my life, I've started my photography business, I'm baking cakes and working at the hospital and enjoying life, I have my first grandchild it cannot get any better than this. Philippians 4:6, Be careful about nothing; but in everything by prayer and supplication with thanksgiving let your requests be made known unto God. This was my new motto, through prayer, I was going to let God know what I needed, and I continued to fast and pray and trust God, and he moved for me, now this is what Satan hates when we walk in obedience. Now he's causing division in my family, it's like seeing history repeating itself but all we can do is pray, but I don't give the devil what he wants I still call my kids, and siblings and check on them. You cannot provide the devil that much room to destroy your family. Some people cannot see that, because they have hardened their hearts that are filled with unforgiveness and yet they lie on God and say God told them to disown or separate from their loved ones. Now don't get me wrong sometimes God will move people out of your life but when you come to Christ, you can discern that negative unforgiven spirit. Whatever God does he do with love even if he is stern with us? Somethings has nothing to do with God it's us, I know because that was me that was my way of not letting people in who had hurt me get close to me again, people who I just never forgave. When I released all of that it was such a good feeling, I felt terrific. I try to look at the positive side of things not the negative stuff now because now I know who the author of confusion is I had to learn to find peace and love within myself through Christ to get where I needed to be in Christ. My sister taught me how to fast, and that was one of the best things I could have done, I began to really see GOD move in my life and now I can hear his voice. I also started to have a lot of dreams, dreams that I knew meant something that was spiritual, and one particular that really changed my life was, I remember I was cleaning my house sweeping and listing to music in this dream, and I heard a loud trumpet sound, and I knew that Jesus was coming. My kids were in there rooms playing with their toys I could hear them. So I looked out my door, and the sky had opened up, and I saw beautiful white horses and chariots coming down with beautiful angels guiding them.

Going everywhere, so I closed the
door and really began to cry out to
GOD and repent, then I heard a
knock on my door it was so loud,
and when I opened it, it was a
beautiful angel with a golden scroll
in his hand, and he said ... Brandon,
Chris, Brittney, and Carey. I looked
at him and said can you please check
to see if my name is on there... so
he opened it up and nodded his head
no, I ask him was he sure and he
then spoke to me and said, are you
ready to get real and stop playing
with GOD? Maybe you'll be
prepared for his second coming, my
kids ran out the room, and I watch
my kids in the back of the chariot
smiling and playing with each other

and so happy but looking at me like mommy why are you not coming. As I looked at them because I began to hear so much chaos, I saw Satan standing there laughing so hard at me. Just waiting to get at me he was actually rolling around all over my porch laughing at me that I was left behind. They had people getting beheaded all over my neighborhood, Satan had so many demons working with him, and they all looked deformed, I slammed my door and began to cry but it was too late I was left behind. GOD has a way of getting our attention that's for sure, I still have my struggles, but that dream always gets me right back where I need to be.

Chapter 5

GOING WITH MY FEELINGS AGAIN

Hebrews 11:1 Now, faith is the substance of things hoped for, the evidence of things not seen. One thing as a child of the king you will learn, and that is without faith you will not please GOD, why because you cannot walk in fear, you cannot doubt, you must trust GOD with everything that is in you to receive from GOD. How do you increase your faith? By reading your word and meditating on it day and night. Let it get in your heart and soul, and that comes by reading your word and believing what you have read to be true knowing that GOD cannot lie. I have learned that when I have a problem now, and I don't know what to do, or things look bad for me, I give it to GOD and leave it there. Now, I have not always done that I was a worry wart at one time and sometimes I still have to go to GOD and pray for an increase of my faith. Over the years, of course, my faith has been tested, and it's been hard, I married again, WHY?? Because I went off my feelings and it has not been easy, we have a blended family although it's just his two kids that live with us it's been very hard. We relocated because of issues we were having, and still, we are struggling why? Because we have decreased our prayer life and allowed the enemy to come in and rob us of what we are supposed to do for GOD. And GOD told me not to relocate back to Louisiana, and I did, my husband went from a man that prayed day and night to one that drinks and party all night until the next day. My husband began to let his kids run his life he forgot what comes first in his life and this is not something I could stand for, GOD is always first. We have only been married two years, and trust is already broken, infidelity, lies and separation and of course Satan is happy he thinks he's won, but I refuse to allow myself waste time living with anyone who won't live for GOD. You can't love me if you don't love GOD. I don't feel you love GOD if you can disrespect him the way you disregarded His Word when it said a husband and wife are one. Because loving God means honoring him not allowing your kids, friends, family, etc...To disrespect you, your spouse and what you believe in as a man of GOD. Most of all I don't like being 50 being treated for an STD because my husband continually cheats and then blame it on drinking and partying. When I met him, he walked around with a bible in his hand, this is not the same person, this person is drunk all the time, so we can't really blame the kids or family or anyone in our relationships because if they see our spouse not respecting us, how can they? My husband was actually entertaining his family and friends talking about me. He admitted that much at our counseling where his pastor did tell him that he was allowing his kids to destroy his marriage. Basically, because pictures that were posted on social media was found in his kid's phone that they did post. My last Christmas with him he told me that his, friends said, if it were them they wouldn't buy me anything, and I just looked at him, you know what that said to me that not only he was still talking about me and being disrespectful to me, but he was allowing his friends to do the same. Women of GOD this is not GOD!!! It was time to go and that day I made up my mind to do so, and that was the best choice for us because he didn't have my back, he did not protect me, he did not cover me, and we never prayed together anymore. I prayed alone, and GOD moved on my behalf. I was at work, and the Holy Spirit spoke to me and said, as long as you allow him to treat you that way he will it's time to go. At first, I was confused but the next day I received a phone call from the Man of GOD, and he said sis GOD told me to call you and tell you as long as you allow him to treat you that way he will it's time to separate. What confused me was I stayed single, and I kept myself for years until I met him. I really tried to wait on God because I didn't want my husband to ever worry about someone being with his wife or me just being an ungodly woman. He was just the opposite he was not worried about my feeling, I couldn't go anywhere without someone knowing him the party animal, and seeing him on social media drunk with different women some younger than his kids and old he didn't have the respect of person I guess.

It was embarrassing and humiliating, it was time to go. Women you don't

have to settle for this. I had to buy
my own food and pay my own bills.
So, I felt like what did I need him
for, and I remember one day asking
him what he wanted for dinner. I
was going to cook what he had in
the freezer, and he told me not to
touch it, it was for his girls, so now I
couldn't eat what he buys for him
and them., Ok, I get it and of course
he said later he didn't mean it like
that. He continued to shop for only
them and with his kids. We did
nothing together anymore it was
crazy. I was accused of stealing
clothes that I couldn't fit I mean
crazy stuff and whatever he was told
about me he believed, and he
checked me out about it and believe

it. So, I had a husband who not only did not support me but did not believe in me at all, and I had not done anything to deserve this treatment it was crazy. Ladies, I'm not saying for no one to do what I did, pray about it because God may tell you something different. I left because I refused to be disrespected and lied on. Most of all watch my husband play with the GOD who gave his life for you and me on the cross. Ephesians 5:22, 23, 25, says Wives, submit yourselves unto your own husbands, as unto the Lord. For the husband is the head of the wife, even as Christ is the head of the church: and he is the savior of the body. 25, Husbands, love your wives, even as Christ also loved the church, and gave himself for it; Once again, I went with my feelings, I thought I could handle anything, I thought I was stronger. I was receiving threatening messages from his daughter on Facebook, which I saved, I had DHS at my door, it was nonstop drama. Then I grew angry and bitter and stop my focus on GOD and made it about me and my feelings and about what people were doing to me again and I didn't want to go back to where I fought so hard to get away from. One day at work and thinking I know I had to leave my husband because I refuse to waste my time with a man who didn't love me. He didn't love me

enough to love me the way GOD
ordained it to be I started feeling
sorry for myself like I had failed
again and I had tried to do
everything right and immediately
I heard GOD speak very clearly to
me… and he said…who are you that
people can't lie on you and hurt you
and do you wrong who are you???
I just look around to see who all was
watching me because I was having a
pity party with myself. Crying
because I did not deserve this
treatment I was receiving from my
husband. GOD ministered to my
heart, and he said, they lied on me,
they spit on me, they beat me, they
crucified me, and who are you? Are
you greater than I am? I began to

weep and repent and ask for forgiveness. However, I still made the decision to leave after I heard from GOD, but I knew I had to forgive, and the enemy wanted me to feel like a failure, this was my third marriage, and I vowed again after this, I would just stay single it's too hard and hurtful. I had a husband who I felt don't love me, he loves the things of this world much more and like so many other men I saw were lovers of this world and playing with GOD, and I just was not settling for that. I just finished ministry school and I had no support from him at all and it was a struggle for me. My health was terrible I was sick all the time I started having seizures passing out everything was happening I was so stressed, and all I kept hearing from my doctor was you need to take an antidepressant because stress can kill you, well that made it worst. But When I move and left him all my symptoms left, I didn't want the health issues my mom had so I began to change everything my eating habits. I started going to the gym and putting change into motion leaving that toxic marriage and I felt good. I lost 60 lbs. in 6 months, and I began to feel better, I stop letting things bother me, I also didn't make a move without GOD this time I always was a runner I would just move when things would get rough but I was not doing that I was going to hear from GOD clearly and not anyone else. Yes, my mind was made up because I knew I wanted better and my husband didn't want to change. I wanted someone I could grow in Christ with that could pray me through some things and I could do the same for him, but he became a worldly person at this point. When I needed him the most, and I feel like we're living in the end times, and we can't play with salvation we must live totally for Christ, we can't be Luke warm. I must say I don't regret anything I went through still because if I never married him, I would have never experienced love inside of me that I had not before because I didn't know how to really forgive until I met him. To love in spite of everything I when through. I still did everything for him as his wife, and it was not hard because I loved GOD so much. In the past I wasn't right I was selfish in my past relationships, and it was all about me, but this was different for me. I loved him unconditionally, and I stayed and tried harder than I ever thought I would. But on December 26, 2017, I received a phone call from a man of GOD, and he asked me how I was doing.

I said fine as usual, and he said no you're not, but GOD said as long as you allow your husband to treat you that way he will. He is taking you for granted, but you are about to get a phone call he said, at this point, I'm looking really confused at this point. He said you put in for a job a while ago, but they did not call you because you were not ready to go, but God says you're ready now your mind is made up your tired you had enough now he's opening doors for you and this job will pay much more than your, post now. Two days later I received a phone call from an unknown number I started not to answer, but I did. The lady on the phone said... Mrs. Thomas … I said yes, she said you put in an application back in October with us, and I don't know how we over overlooked yours but are you still interested? Of course, I said yes, and two days later I was on the next flight, took the job came backpacked up all my stuff from the apartment I shared with my husband turned in the key told him goodbye. He thought I was going by my daughter to stay, but I had left Louisiana and moved and started my new job the pay is incredible the people are good GOD is good.

I have no regrets!!! Everything is a learning experience, and a lesson learned a testimony. I'm stronger because of it, and now I can help others and share my knowledge about going off feelings. I'm not going to say it was all great when I came here because I totally had shut down from everyone, I had never experienced that much hurt and pain in my life from loving someone and I did not want to talk about it, and I didn't. I changed my, phone number I cut everybody off except my kids and siblings and two ministers from my church. My best friend Sandra oh my goodness Sandra has always been there for me I remember when I was young she was going to try to help me run away, but my mom caught us, so that did not go over too well. How do we get to focus on God and his purpose for us? Well, I had to do a lot of praying because

when I first moved the enemy was
telling me that I was going through
this because of everything I had
done wrong in my life and that I was
still being punished. I cried every
day for two months, and finally I
talked to my son about what was
bothering me, and he said mom that
is not how GOD works, he doesn't
want you to keep suffering and he
forgave you already. I was so
relieved I thank GOD for Little
Carey, he motivates me so much
spiritually, but I don't think he
realizes it, my daughter also she is a
fantastic support team. I knew I was
writing this book so I began to save

and document everything, every photo that was taken of me every video every ugly facebook message I received, I kept it all because I did not trust him or them. But my storm is over now because GOD had a plan and a purpose for me.

CHAPTER 6

FOCUSING ON MY PURPOSE AND PRAYER LIFE

It's no time for pity parties on why this happened to me or why anything, it's now time to focus on what is it I am to do for my Lord and Savior. If I hadn't gone through anything,, I wouldn't be able to help others and be able to relate… so no regret. Now it's time to focus on what I am supposed to do, and what's my purpose in life?

I had to first realize everything was not my parent's fault, they were not a mistake, GOD chose them for me for a reason, and I love them. GOD made no mistakes in my life it was all for my purpose. Because things did not go the way, I planned or thought it should don't mean it's not going the way it should or was mapped out to be. I am not an accident nor was I a mistake I am here for a reason, and my life went the way it did for a reason. It's not about me. Some things I went through was because of my own disobedience, and some were to help others. Everything we go through is a learning process for you to grow and mature in the knowledge of GOD. Mistakes I've made in the past I have learned from them. One of my purpose on this earth is to help other women and young mothers not to make the same mistakes I have made by not waiting on GOD. Also realizing that GOD can speak to you just like anybody else. I would call Prophet Ayers all the time but he told me you know Sis you can go to GOD and He will talk to you just like He talks to me if you're sincere, but you must have faith. GOD loves us all the same, unconditionally and we all have choices in life, it's up to us what road we choose. But remember that some of the choices we make can have an effect on others that we love dearly, and somethings we can't take back, therefore choose your words wisely because there is power in the tongue. I spoke a lot of stuff on myself not knowing it. I learned just how deadly the tongue is, and it's a lot of things I wish I could take back but I can't. No regrets, it was a learning experience, someone asked me is there anything I would've done differently in my life if given a chance? No none I learned something from everything I been through, every relationship, trial, and the mistake was indeed a learning process, and I wouldn't be who I am today if had not gone through any of it. Now did I have to go through all the heartache? No, I went through because of my disobedience, I'm sure GOD plan for me was a lot greater. I've learned to pray before I make a move and except my wrong and how not to make the same again. I have a lot of things in life that I want to do but, I will not make a move on my own anymore.

CHAPTER 7

GOD IS A HEALER, HE IS FAITHFUL, POWERFUL HE IS LOVE

Three things happened to me that stood out in my life that I will never forget. First I want to say that I have experienced GOD power first hand and he is awesome. I remembered being pregnant and had a terrible toothache it was like 3am in the morning, so I called my sister and walked over to her house, and she anointed her hands and asked me if I believe GOD can heal me? Now, I had only been saved a short time, but I had faith. I believed if two or more were together GOD was there. He would heal me because I had read it in my bible, so I told her yes I believe. She laid her hands on my jaw where a toothache was, and I felt a heat wave go through my face, and that pain subsided instantly. I was so happy not only I knew how real GOD was and he loved me enough that he didn't let me suffer any longer. I laughed, I cried, when I ate her grapes I was so hungry. Second time, GOD showed up, was in 2016. I had a Mammogram, and it showed two mass on my left breast had another done show the same thing. I had a couple of people praying with me because I had allowed the enemy to put fear in me, I could feel this thing, and I let my daughter and others feel it who I shared it with. After my second test, I went to my doctor appointment a couple of days later, and my doctor asked me to show her where I felt it at. When I did it was no longer there, now that morning it was there, now my doctor sent me to get another mammogram and an ultrasound of my breast, and they couldn't find anything. GOD IS A HEALER, that same year I had an MRI because I would have dizzy spells, well they found white matter on the brain which is common.

My doctor felt because of what he saw I needed another one done, and I did, and when I went saw him the next week he said I had a brain of a 70-year-old. Ok now, I'm too young for that and I know a man who is a healer and his name is JESUS he has done it to many times for me and I trust him, I was sent to a specialist and had a third one did which showed absolutely signs of dementia and no white matter on the brain. GOD has been too good for me not to give him my all. In closing, I would like to say again that I don't want to offend anyone. Just to help someone, not to blame no one but to give strength to someone.

To let GOD people know that its so important that we wait on him for everything, especially if you don't know what to do don't do anything. Just wait, and please if you holding any bitterness in heart for anyone let it go. And remember that Satan knows the word and how to quote scriptures.

Closing Remarks

To all the women that move before God told you to move it was not your divine purpose in your disobedience. But I believe in second chances, and if you let God order your footsteps you will find that divine purpose God placed in you!!!!

Second Chances

Lamentations 3:21-23 "But this I call to mind, and therefore I have hope: The steadfast love of the Lord never ceases; his mercies never come to an end; they are new every morning; great is your faithfulness."

Closing Remarks

To my kids:
Brandon, Chris, Brittney,
and Carey. Let God order
your footsteps so that you
all will find that divine
purpose God place in each
one of you!!!!

Michelle T. Duplessis

I MAY HAVE BEEN
BRUISE, BUT I WAS
NOT BROKEN

Made in the USA
Lexington, KY
09 June 2019